CCSS Genre Folktale

Essential Question
How can we understand nature?

MW00713868

Why Spider Has 8 Thin Legs

by Jana Higgins

illustrated by Jeremy Tugeau

Scene 1
Anansi Is Hungry!......................2

Scene 2
Anansi's New Legs...................11

Scene 3
Feast with Friends 14

Respond to Reading.................16

PAIRED READ **Why There Are Stars**..........17

Focus on Literary Elements..........20

Scene 1: Anansi Is Hungry!

SETTING: An African village, a long time ago

Anansi the Spider: After weaving all of these webs today, I am tired and very hungry. I am also really sick of eating flies. I think I will dash around the village and see what my neighbors are preparing for lunch! I am certain they have something delicious on the fire.

Anansi the Spider: Yum, Rabbit! Those vegetables smell fantastic. I'm sure they will be very tasty, and I am so terribly hungry today.

Rabbit: They are almost ready, and yes, they will be delicious. Why don't you stay here and eat with us?

Anansi the Spider: I can't stay, but please take this thread and pull it when the vegetables are ready.

Anansi the Spider: Hello, Monkey! That banana pudding looks really yummy! I am so hungry I can hear my stomach rumbling.

Monkey: I am almost done cooking it, so please stay and eat with my family, Anansi!

Anansi the Spider: I can't stay, but take this thread and pull it when the pudding is ready.

Anansi the Spider: Hello, Hog! Those beans look good enough to eat!

Hog: I am making beans for our dinner. I don't like to boast, but everyone in the village says I make the best beans in the whole world! Would you like to eat some?

Anansi the Spider: I can't stay, but take this thread and pull it when the beans are ready.

Anansi the Spider: Hello, Lion! I am hungry for the spicy stew you are cooking up!

Lion: This stew has been cooking all day, but now it is almost ready. Why don't you sit down and enjoy some stew with me, Anansi?

Anansi the Spider: I can't stay, but take this thread and pull it when the stew is ready.

Anansi the Spider: Hello, Turtle! That berry mash looks like it would taste so sweet.

Turtle: It is sweet because I put honey and spices in it. Perhaps you would like to taste the berries? They will be delicious.

Anansi the Spider: I can't stay, but take this thread and pull it when the berries are ready.

Anansi the Spider: Hello, Elephant! I love tasty lettuce leaves, and I can't help but notice that you are making my favorite green salad.

Elephant: Yes, I am! My salad is crunchy and has carrots in it. I have used the history and wisdom of my family to learn how to prepare it. Would you like to eat some?

Anansi the Spider: I can't stay, but take this thread and pull it when the salad is ready.

Anansi the Spider: Hello, Rhino! Your turnip soup smells so good, it is making my mouth water! Will it be ready soon?

Rhino: It only needs to cook for a few more minutes. Would you like to sit down and enjoy a bowl of soup with me, dear friend?

Anansi the Spider: I can't stay, but take this thread and pull it when the soup is ready.

Anansi the Spider: Hello up there, Giraffe! Those banana leaves look so fresh that I would like to eat some if that is possible!

Giraffe: They are absolutely delicious, Anansi. I will put rice in the leaves and roll them up. Would you like to stay here and have some?

Anansi the Spider: I can't stay, but please take this thread and pull it when the banana leaves are ready.

SETTING: By the river

Anansi the Spider: I am hungrier than ever! I wish the food had been ready when I visited each of my neighbors. Well, at least I was clever enough to attach the web threads to my legs. I am sure the food will be ready very soon. I will know when I feel the threads pull on my legs.

Anansi the Spider: Oh, my goodness! The threads are pulling my legs, which means all of the food must be ready. My legs feel so strange that I feel like I might holler! I'm sorry I was so greedy!

Anansi the Spider: But look at my legs! They are all stretched out, so I can run faster and spin threads more quickly! My new thin legs make me very happy. I'm going to walk back to the village and show my neighbors my new legs. If they share some of their food with me, I won't be greedy.

SETTING: Back in the village

Hog: Hey, everyone, take a look at Anansi's legs!

Giraffe: Your legs are almost as long as mine!

Turtle: Wow, Anansi! I wish my legs were long like yours!

Anansi the Spider: When each of you pulled the threads I gave you, my legs stretched and got longer. Now I can run fast and spin webs more quickly. What a victory for me!

Elephant: Anansi, please join us for a wonderful feast! My salad is delicious!

Rabbit: Each of us brought our dishes to share, so please have some vegetables.

Monkey: I brought banana pudding, and Hog made beans.

Lion: My stew is nice and spicy, and Turtle's berry mash is sweet!

Rhino: Try some of my turnip soup, and don't forget the salad and banana leaves.

Anansi the Spider: Thank you for sharing with me! I have the best friends in the world!

Summarize

Use important details to summarize *Why Spider Has 8 Thin Legs*.

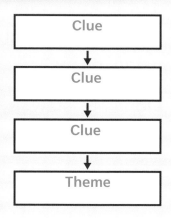

Clue

↓

Clue

↓

Clue

↓

Theme

Text Evidence

1. How do you know *Why Spider Has 8 Thin Legs* is a folktale? GENRE

2. How does the reader find out why spiders have eight thin legs? Use details to support your answer. THEME

3. Use what you know about root words to figure out the meaning of *sharing* on page 15. ROOT WORDS

4. Write about why it is not good to be greedy. Use details about what happened to Anansi to support your answer. WRITE ABOUT READING

Compare Texts

Read to find out why there are stars in the sky.

Why There Are STARS

A long, long time ago, a young girl lived with her mother in a village far away. This girl was a stubborn girl. You might even say she was a bit spoiled. In other words, she was very used to getting her own way.

17

One day the girl's mother was cooking over an open fire. The mother was roasting tasty vegetables that have some similarities to sweet potatoes. These vegetables were absolutely delicious! The girl ate plate after plate full of them. She wanted more, but her mother told her she had eaten plenty.

Illustration: Ivica Stevanovic

The girl was so angry that she grabbed the vegetables from the fire and threw the ashes into the sky. Then her hands hurt from grabbing the hot vegetables. Right away, the girl was ashamed of her bad behavior.

But the story has a happy ending! The red and white ashes floated up high. They became the red and white stars of the Milky Way. And that is why there are stars in the sky.

Make Connections

How does the folktale explain why there are stars in the sky? ESSENTIAL QUESTION

How do these two folktales tell how different cultures explain the natural world? TEXT TO TEXT

Focus on Literary Elements

Theme The theme is the life lesson or message in a story or play.

What to Look for Look for the parts in the beginning and end of the folktale that explain why spiders have thin legs. Notice how spider feels about being greedy. See how his friends forgive him.

Your Turn

Imagine you are writing a folktale. You can write about why the moon comes out at night or something else in nature. Make a list and describe the characters that your folktale would include. Decide what the setting would be like. Finally, think about what lesson you want people to learn. Draw a few pictures to go with the folktale, and write captions for your pictures.